Images of War
Afrika-Korps

Images of War
Afrika-Korps

Ian Baxter

Pen & Sword
MILITARY

First published in Great Britain in 2008 by
PEN & SWORD MILITARY
an imprint of
Pen & Sword Books Ltd,
47 Church Street,
Barnsley,
South Yorkshire.
S70 2AS

A CIP record for this book is available from the British Library.

ISBN 978 1 84415 6 832

Printed and bound by CPI UK

Pen & Sword Books Ltd incorporates the Imprints of
Pen & Sword Aviation, Pen & Sword Maritime,
Pen & Sword Military, Wharncliffe Local History, Pen & Sword Select,
Pen & Sword Military Classics and Leo Cooper.

For a complete list of Pen & Sword titles please contact
Pen & Sword Books Limited
47 Church Street, Barnsley, South Yorkshire, S70 2AS, England
E-mail: enquiries@pen-and-sword.co.uk
Website: www.pen-and-sword.co.uk

Contents

Introduction

Afrika-Korps is an illustrated record of Field-Marshal Erwin Rommel and his desert troops that fought in North Africa against British, Commonwealth and American forces between 1941 and 1943. Using rare and previously unpublished photographs, many of which have come from the albums of individuals who took part in the desert campaign, it presents a unique visual account of Rommel and his Afrika-Korps. With an informative caption for every photograph, Afrika-Korps vividly portrays how the German Army fought across the uncharted and forbidding desert wilderness of North Africa, and describes how Erwin Rommel finally stamped his greatest achievements in the desert, making him a living legend to this day.

Throughout the book it examines how Rommel and his Afrika-Korps became successful and includes an analysis of desert war tactics with which Rommel himself had indoctrinated his troops. These tactics quickly won the Afrika-Korps a string of victories between 1941 and 1942, and are all the more remarkable as they were won when the Germans were often outnumbered and at the end of their supply lines.

The photographs that accompany the book are an interesting assortment that depicts life in the Afrika-Korps, as seen through the lens of the ordinary soldier. Throughout the book the images, accompanied by detailed captions, show how the Germans in the desert conducted their military operations attuned to the Blitzkrieg style of warfare. It reveals how these elite desert troops fought with vigour and determination, frequently fighting a more numerous and powerful enemy.

Photographic Acknowledgements

It is with the greatest pleasure that I use this opportunity on concluding this book to thank those who helped make this volume possible. My expression of gratitude first goes to my German photographic collector Rolf Halfen. He has been an unfailing source, supplying me with a number of photographs that were obtained from numerous private sources. Throughout the research stage of this book Rolf searched and contacted numerous collectors all over Germany, trying, sometimes in vain, to find a multitude of interesting and rare photographs.

Further afield in Poland, I am also extremely grateful to Marcin Kaludow, my Polish photographic specialist, who supplied me with a variety of photographs that he sought from private photographic collections in Poland.

Finally, I wish to display my gratitude and appreciation to my American photographic collector, Richard White, who supplied me with a number of rare unpublished photographs, especially the various photographs of Rommel and his staff.

All other images in this book are credited to the HITM ARCHIVE
www.hitm-archive.co.uk

The Author

Ian Baxter is a military historian who specialises in German twentieth century military history. He has written more than twenty books including 'Wolf' Hitler's Wartime Headquarters, Poland – The Eighteen Day Victory March, Panzers In North Africa, The Ardennes Offensive, The Western Campaign, The 12th SS Panzer-Division Hitlerjugend, The Waffen-SS on the Western Front, The Waffen-SS on the Eastern Front, The Red Army at Stalingrad, Elite German Forces of World War II, Armoured Warfare, German Tanks of War, Blitzkrieg, Panzer-Divisions at War, Hitler's Panzers, German Armoured Vehicles of World War Two, Last Two Years of the Waffen-SS at War, German Soldier Uniforms and Insignia, German Guns of the Third Reich, Defeat to Retreat: The Last Years of the German Army at War 1943 – 1945, Biography of Rudolf Hoss, Operation Bagration – the destruction of Army Group Centre, and most recently The Afrika-Korps. He has written over one hundred journals including 'Last days of Hitler, Wolf's Lair, Story of the V1 and V2 Rocket Programme, Secret Aircraft of World War Two, Rommel at Tobruk, Hitler's War with his Generals, Secret British Plans to Assassinate Hitler, SS at Arnhem, Hitlerjugend, Battle of Caen 1944, Gebirgsjäger at War, Panzer Crews, Hitlerjugend Guerrillas, Last Battles in the East, Battle of Berlin', and many more. He has also reviewed numerous military studies for publication and supplied thousands of photographs and important documents to various publishers and film production companies worldwide.

Chapter One

Afrika-Korps Arrival

By the time that the order came through from Berlin to the German military command in late 1940 there had been no thorough preparations to send German troops to North Africa. Nonetheless the Germans soon got down to detailed planning. There was a large selection of all troops deemed medically fit to fight in the desert. Masses of equipment and tropical uniforms, together with a variety of vehicles camouflaged with sand paint, were quickly readied for North Africa. Training programmes too were distributed among the new troops, which included subjects such as operating in extreme heat across vast areas of terrain and coping with the harsh conditions. There was even a section that dealt with field hygiene and water discipline.

Once the new Afrika-Korps were prepared for operations in North Africa the first part of the journey for the men was normally overland to Italy and then they were transported either by air or by sea. Most troops, during the initial stages of arrival in the port of Tripoli, were transported by sea, but when shipping losses increased, all transport was eventually carried out by air only.

On 14 February 1941 the first troops of the elite Afrika-Korps sailed into the port of Tripoli. That night thousands of tons of equipment, ranging from guns and armoured vehicles to tents and mosquito netting, were unloaded off onto the flood-lit dockside in spite of the risk of an aerial attack.

The next day a military parade was held in the town watched by bewildered groups of Arabs and Italians. Under the baking African sun the vanguard of the Afrika-Korps, clad in their new tropical uniforms with pith helmets, marched flawlessly passed the government house, with General Erwin Rommel and a group of Italian generals standing by his side taking the salute. This would be the first of many such military parades as the build-up of German soldiers increased.

Over the next days and weeks, further ships and aircraft brought more fresh men and equipment and disembarked with the usual propaganda parade. With crowds cheering and the German and Italian national anthems playing, the main roads through the Libyan capital were brought to life by the spectacle of endless columns of rattling German tanks of the 5th Light and 3rd Panzer Regiments. To the waving spectators there seemed no end to this armoured military might, for Rommel had in fact cleverly ordered the tanks to drive around the block to give the impression of a large army. He was determined, telling the Panzer Regiments' officers that until the rest of the force arrived, they were to 'bluff' their way into North Africa, and not show the enemy their weakness. To add to this measure of deception he had ordered his troops to build hundreds of dummy tanks, constructed out of plywood and canvas, in order to fool air reconnaissance. Out in the desert this so called 'staged army' was surrounded by real trucks and motorcyclists driving in and around them, with real tanks churning tracks across the sand for enemy planes to spot them and take photographs.

Almost none of the soldiers had actually fought in the desert before, and many of them did not really know what to expect. For any soldier fighting in North Africa, conditions would not be very favourable. They would have to endure the enormous distances which they had to travel especially during the scorching days and chilling nights, and would be subjected to frequent blinding sandstorms. To make matters worse they not only had to trudge through this open wilderness, naked to the enemy, but they had the hazards of the desert sand-choking valuable machines and equipment. They also had to contend with the rarity of water, and the great strain on vehicles from wear and tear.

The terrain factor for the newly arrived Afrika-Korps was not considered very favourable, especially under battle conditions. Immediately though, General Rommel set to work from his headquarters in Tripoli and made good use of what he had at his disposal. The lack of terrain obstacles and the supply difficulties were all taken into consideration. Unlike in Poland and Western Europe Rommel was totally aware that, with the exception of a few isolated fortified localities in towns and villages, there were no long defensive lines that existed which he could probe to find weak spots for penetration and exploitation. However, Rommel had earned his reputation against France as a great tactician, and now in North Africa would use the same rough principles with his new Panzer force to destroy the enemy using tried and tested Blitzkrieg tactics. Rommel planned to use his force to advance across the desert in several columns, with the Panzers being concentrated in one or two columns. A battalion of 70 or 80 tanks were to use a 'V' formation with two companies leading and one in reserve. Across the desert the tank battalion would be used in short rushes, taking full advantage of the terrain, with lines of spaced out Panzers advancing quickly in waves. Both field artillery and anti-tank guns were to be kept in close support of the advancing armour and were used to protect the flanks and keep open the spearhead.

In spite of Rommel's methodical planning and tactics to be used on the battlefield, his force arrived in Tripoli almost completely unprepared for their new task. However, initially the newly formed Afrika-Korps were to be used as an armoured blocking force to bolster the badly depleted and shattered forces of the Italian Army in Tripolitania and prevent further British advances. Any plans Rommel had of using his German force in an offensive campaign in the desert was ruled out, if only for the time being. Instead the General had to watch impatiently as his African force was slowly built up, whilst at the same time observing the situation out in the desert deteriorating further.

By mid-March 1941 only 150 Panzers had been unloaded in Tripoli harbour, of which most were the lightly armoured Pz.Kpfw.I. By this time Rommel could no longer wait and watch the campaign worsen any further. He now gathered his troops for an offensive in the desert.

February 1941 and many transport ships can be seen anchored in the port of Tripoli following the first dispatch of German troops to North Africa. The first troops were comprised of advanced echelon troops of the 5th Light and 3rd Panzer Regiments as well as reconnaissance soldiers and support units.

Two photographs showing the same transport ship, which has arrived in the port of Tripoli after it had sailed across the hazardous Mediterranean. Throughout 1941 the British began waging an intense and relentless war against enemy transport ships and supplies travelling from Italy and Libya. Moreover, dock installations at the port of Tripoli were limited and could not allow the unloading of more than four or five ships at a time. Therefore in order to increase the amount of shipping, further ports along the coast were to be secured and defended with the aid of the Italian Air Force.

German troops wait at the dockside to receive more supplies for the campaign in North Africa. During the initial stages of the Afrika-Korps arrival the bulk of supplies were brought to the shores of Libya by vessel. However, when shipping losses increased, all transport was eventually undertaken by air transport.

A halftrack being hoisted onto the dockside using the ships crane. A number of the vehicles that actually arrived in North Africa during the initial stages of the campaign had not received a coating of sand camouflage paint. By the time the order came through in late 1940 there had been no thorough preparation to send German troops to North Africa and as a consequence some vehicles arrived in Tripoli still retaining their overall dark grey camouflage schemes.

Two photographs showing a Pz.Kpfw.III being carefully lowered by the ships crane onto the dockside. Throughout the campaign in North Africa, especially during 1941 and 1942, the Pz.Kpfw.III demonstrated its effectiveness of overrunning enemy positions with speed and manoeuvrability, and used its gun as artillery against forward enemy columns with devastating effect. With such success this particular Panzer type was used as the main striking force in the North Africa and had a dominant role in anti-tank combat.

A German Flak 2cm gunner protects the port of Tripoli against aerial attacks, whilst three Italian soldiers can be seen posing for the camera. Whilst the Germans were building their forces the Italians too were undergoing some major changes in order to strengthen its badly depleted army. In April 1941 the Italian troops fielded the newly arrived Ariete Armoured Division.

A soldier belonging to the newly arrived Afrika-Korps rests onboard a transport ship during the initial stages of the Germans sending supplies to Tripoli in February and March 1941. Note the stacks of sand bags. Literally thousands of sand bags were transported to North Africa and used widely throughout the campaign for protection against the harsh environment and defensive positions.

A 2cm Flak gunner protects the port of Tripoli against the threat of aerial attacks by the British. The 2cm Flak gun was a successful anti-aircraft weapon that was used widely during the African campaign.

Another method of transporting vital men and equipment to North Africa was by aircraft. Here Junker 52s pass over the Libyan coastline. This single engine transport aeroplane of the Luftwaffe was very reliable and became the main form of supply from Italy to North Africa. However, very vulnerable to fighter attack an escort was always necessary when flying in a combat zone. Many Ju 52s were shot down by anti-aircraft guns and fighters while transporting their supplies.

A Pz.Kpfw.II being lifted off a transport ship onto the dockside at Tripoli. Large numbers of the Pz.Kpfw.II's were to eventually see action in North Africa. However, it was soon realized that these light Panzers were under-gunned and suffered from very thin armour, which offered the crews minimal protection from battle.

Pz.Kpfw.IIs and Pz.Kpfw.Is have been unloaded at the dockside in Tripoli and the crews can be seen preparing their machines. The vehicles still retain their 1940 dark grey camouflage paint, and belong to the 5th Light Division. These Panzers arrived in Libya still carrying the 3rd Panzer Division markings, as can be identified by the yellow inverted 'Y' and two yellow marks painted on the rear of the tanks' offside fenders.

From a flak gun position the photograph shows the various vehicles and equipment unloaded at the dockside. Over the coming days and weeks thousands of tons of equipment, ranging from guns and armoured vehicles to tents and mosquito nets, were unloaded in spite of the constant dangers of aerial attack.

One of the most successful flak guns of World War Two is being carefully unloaded onto the dockside. The 8.8cm Flak gun was widely used by the Afrika-Korps in both an anti-tank and anti-aircraft role. It scored sizable successes against the British and became a very much feared weapon.

Two soldiers are seen here driving through the desert during the initial stages of the campaign in North Africa. The passenger wears the Luftwaffe tropical helmet whilst the driver can be seen wearing Zeiss goggles. The dust and sand was a constant problem in the desert and many soldiers, especially whilst driving, took to wearing goggles, even captured ones.

Here an Opel Maultier towing a 10.5cm le. FH 18 can be seen leaving the nose ramp of a Messerschmitt 323 'Gigant' transport plane. By mid 1941 the bulk of supplies were being transported by air.

Four soldiers of the Afrika-Korps rest in the desert. Their rifles are stacked together in this way to avoid dust and dirt getting into the firing mechanism and so that they are quickly accessible if they are urgently required to go into action.

A soldier who holds the rank of a Gefreiter poses in his German Army tropical field service uniform in 1941. The service uniform dyed in a light sage-green colour and the trousers are tucked in the special leather high lace-up tropical boots. He also wears tropical pith helmet, which was issued to most German soldier all ranks during this period of the war. However, it was not a popular item of clothing. The soldier also wears a shirt and tie gives a formal appearance, which is in marked contrast to the typical desert wear used by the Afrika-Korps.

Afrika-Korps troops, dressed in their familiar tropical greatcoats out in the Libyan Desert, pose for the camera next to their vehicle heavily laden with supplies. The long distances which these vehicles had to travel, over hundreds of miles of sandy and rough terrain, were a trip that many soldiers never forgot.

Two Junker JU52 transporters are seen here halted on a makeshift airfield in the desert. Regular daily flights were made by these aircraft in order to keep the supply lines open.

A Horch cross-country car has stopped in the desert. The driver can be seen standing next to his vehicle whilst the officers are still seated in the back.

A soldier poses for the camera whilst standing in front of a Horch cross-country vehicle. Note that on the vehicle a length of canvas sheeting is protecting the front windshield from the harsh weather conditions out in the desert, which included frequent sandstorms.

A motorcyclist can be seen at one of the many open field stores that littered the desert. He is about to load an army-issue sack, which probably contains mail for the troops. Out in the desert motorcycles were very useful and were able to cover large distances across the arid terrain.

Three vehicles have halted by the roadside. The car leading the drive appears to have water containers or personal equipment attached to the vehicle's roof-rack. Although the Afrika-Korps was supported by numerous water columns during its arduous advance across the desert, troops took drastic measures to ensure they had supplies of their own.

A water field depot out in the middle of the desert. Here vehicles pass through and collect what water they can for their onward journey across the dry, scorching desert. Throughout the campaign water would remain the most important item needed by troops on both sides and great efforts were made to supply the men whatever the danger.

A supply depot out in the desert. These supply lines were the main artery to the Afrika-Korps and ensured that its troops were sustained. However, during 1941 and 1942, Rommel's battlefield tactics often outstripped his supplies, sometimes with dire consequences.

A column of Sd.Kfz.231 heavy armoured cars moves along a road on the sea front in Tripoli in 1941. These vehicles with their long wave radio antennae mounted a 2cm cannon and a 7.92cm MG 34 machine gun for local defence.

Ju52 aircraft have transported troops out into the Libyan Desert near Tripoli in 1941. This was the quickest and most effective means of supplying Rommel's ever-growing African task force.

In front of a tent troops gather around informally to listen to the radio. Tents were the most common feature of desert living in North Africa. They were used not only for living purposes, but also to shelter against the oppressive heat whilst conducting military conferences and other important duties.

An interesting photograph showing what appears to be a soldier belonging to the Sonderverband 288 commandos. These men normally grew long beards and dressed as Arabs whilst operating behind enemy lines.

A captured British vehicle has been pressed into service by an Afrika-Korps signals battalion. Out in the desert, radio communication was an absolute necessity. Armoured signal vehicles almost always accompanied the advance and supplied important communications necessary for the successful conduct of German units fighting out in the desert.

Standing on the rear of a Volkswagen type 82 Kfz.1, a soldier surveys the terrain ahead using a pair of binoculars. With the lack of terrain obstacles, one advantage of desert warfare was the distance in which soldiers could examine the area. Depending on the weather and terrain, soldiers were able to see up to distances of more than 25-miles.

Soldiers belonging to a signals battalion are probably in a forward observation post somewhere east of Tripoli. The signals battalion are using a lightweight radio set and a large 'T' aerial. These were very important pieces of communication equipment and primarily used to send various messages to the divisional headquarters and other chains of command.

Two photographs showing an MG34 machine gun position overlooking positions waiting for the enemy. This machine gun is well sited on top of a rock face and with a well-supplied crew it was more than capable of inflicting very heavy casualties on its enemy. The machine gun's mount also gave the gun sufficient stability to reach a maximum range of 2000 metres.

Two photographs showing soldiers taking various positions among rocks to conceal themselves from the enemy. In photograph 34 an entrenching tool can be seen next to the soldier's foxhole. One of the main problems in selecting a position was the suitability of the area. Quick concealment was often very difficult, especially out in the desert. No doubt this rocky outcrop was a difficult surface to dig.

An anti-tank gunner scans the terrain ahead with a pair of binoculars waiting for the appearance of advancing enemy armour. The anti-tank gun is well concealed beneath its camouflaged netting and would not be easily detectable by the enemy.

A bus from Tripoli has been pressed into service by the Afrika-Korps and used to accommodate soldiers during their drive east. A makeshift tent has been erected over the vehicle and sheeting has been covered across the windscreen in order to reduce the piercing sunrays from entering the compartment. Conditions for the men during the day were often unbearable and shade offered the soldiers the best opportunity to escape from the desert heat.

In a forward observation post a soldier can been seen surveying the battlefield using a pair of scissor binoculars, or 'donkeys ears', as they were commonly known among the men. Just in front of the scissor binoculars is a field telephone.

Two photographs taken of the same Focke-Wulf Fw 189 out in the desert. This twin-engine twin-boom three seat aircraft was nick-named the 'Eagle Owl'. It was a superb tactical reconnaissance aircraft and was used extensively in North Africa between 1941 and 1942. The Fw 189's superb handling and agility made it a very difficult target for attacking British fighters. When attacked, it was quite frequently able to out-turn attacking fighters by simply flying in a tight circle.

Troops are gathered together to listen to their commanding officer during the initial stages of the North African campaign in 1941. Almost none of the soldiers had actually fought in the desert before, and many of them did not really know what to expect. Their commanders, however, were determined to infuse confidence and optimism in them for the coming battle.

For the long duration in the desert, boxes of supplies have been unloaded from a vehicle. The soldiers would soon become aware of the vast distances which they had to travel and the necessity of supplies in such a barren wilderness.

Vehicles can be seen spread out across the desert wilderness as far as the eye can see. For the coming battle in the desert the soldiers would have to endure the constant hazards of the desert sand choking valuable machines and equipment. The constant dust clouds too, created by vehicles moving across the desert, were another problem, as this movement could be detectable from many miles away.

A Pz.Kpfw.35 (t) halted in the desert. These Czech-made Panzers were not extensively used during the North African campaign. It entered service to rival a range of vehicles including the British Vickers 6-ton tank.

Two photographs showing the same anti-tank position during the initial stages of the campaign. The crew can be seen with a 3.7cm Pak anti-tank gun. Note the crew wearing the tropical caps, which are turned back so that they can easily look through the gun sight. Tarpaulin covers the gun. This was done not only to conceal the weapon against advancing armour, but also to protect it against the harsh environment of the desert.

A 21cm Morser being prepared to be moved to a new position. The extensive use of heavy artillery was an important factor to the success of the German drive through Libya. These particular guns were well suited to breaking down heavy defensive positions, especially during the siege of Tobruk later that year.

Having chosen a suitable piece of ground either for defence or attack, soldiers would normally dig and lay sandbags in order to support the unstable walls of the trench. Here in this photograph is a typical German slit trench out in the desert.

Two Pz.Kpfw.IIIs have halted whilst operating east of Tripoli. Note that both vehicles have received an application of sand-colour paint. The main objective of the Pz.Kpfw.III was to knock out the anti-tank guns and all visible field guns.

A photograph taken from an aircraft several hundred feet in the sky, observing a German column of vehicles moving along a road in the desert. Throughout the African campaign constant use was made of both ground and air reconnaissance. As a result of good reconnaissance patrols, German units could not only determine the strength and weakness of the enemy, but also avoid battle when conditions were less favourable.

A photograph taken from a Heinkel 111 shows more Heinkels on an airfield near Tripoli. By this period of the war the Germans had already mastered the art of air-and-ground forces in Blitzkrieg tactics and were now going to unleash this new concept of war on the British in North Africa.

Chapter Two

Rommel As Commander

To the Nazi propaganda machine, during the summer months of 1940, General Erwin Johannes Eugen Rommel had become a charismatic leader whose 'great' 7th Panzer division had victoriously steamrolled through France 'like a ghost fleet'. The propaganda minister Josef Goebbels admired Rommel and went to great lengths in publicising the exploits of his successes against the British and French troops. On the battlefield one officer wrote about Rommel's magic in speed and boldness:

'He shocks the enemy, takes them unawares, overhauls them, suddenly appears far in their rear, attacks them, outflanks them, uses his genius and everything else he's got, taking night and fog and river and obstacle in his stride. Thus his tanks drive long, blooded trails across the map of Europe like the scalpel of a surgeon.'

The French campaign had brought a following among many of the younger officers, and this grew notably during the war. Hundreds were seen flocking from all over Europe, just to glimpse at this classic image of a warrior. To these young soldiers he had become a hero figure. Although the conquering of France had earned Rommel much respect, it would not be until early 1941 in North Africa that he would finally stamp his greatest achievements on the battlefield, which made him a living legend.

On 6 February 1941, after more than seven months of inactivity, General Rommel was summoned to Berlin. In front of Hitler he was told that he had been selected to take command of a small force of two divisions – one Panzer and one light, which was to be sent to Africa in order to help the Italians. Flicking through illustrated magazines with photographs, he read with interest Sir Richard O'Connor's victorious drive into Libya. O'Connor and his two British divisions had advanced 560 miles across the desert to Tobruk and Benghazi, destroying nine Italian divisions, capturing more than 130,000 men and knocking out 845 guns and 380 tanks. With the Italians humiliated, Hitler knew Rommel was probably the only general capable of leading an African force with any type of success. Although Rommel's mission was ostensibly to explore the military situation, he was quite aware, even at this early stage of war planning, that it would be German troops fighting to prevent the British advance through Libya, and not the Italians.

That afternoon, ambitious and determined as ever, Rommel left Berlin with the formal title of Commander-in-Chief of German Troops in Libya. A few weeks later his command would be formally given a new formation title, a name that was to later go down in history, the Deutsches Afrika-Korps, or German Africa Corps.

On 12 February 1941 Rommel boarded his Heinkel bomber and flew to North Africa for the first time. The heat and inhospitable landscape did nothing to inspire this legendary commander of France. Nor did the fact that the Italians were still in full retreat towards the city of Tripoli and were eagerly packing their belongings to catch ships back to Italy before the British arrived. When Rommel arrived in Africa he dined with General Gariboldi and the Italian chief of General Staff, Mario Roatta. Even as they spoke about the deteriorating Italian military position, the vanguard of Rommel's first elite Afrika-Korps troops were already crossing the Mediterranean Sea, bearing down on North Africa. Two days later, on 14 February, passing a wrecked hospital ship, the first troops of the Afrika-Korps sailed into the port of Tripoli. Although at first these units were small, the Afrika-Korps were to become a determined and professional elite, which Rommel was to lead with skill and tenacity. Although the British far outnumbered his small force he had big ambitions for his men. In front of an audience of officers he spoke frankly of the great conquests he was going to win for Germany. 'We're going to advance to the Nile. Then we'll make a right turn and win it all back again!' In a draft letter to Berlin, Rommel noted down his ambitious plans to drive his army 1,500 miles east of Tripoli along the coast until the summer heat prevented any further operations. His first objective was to be the re-conquest of Cyrenaica, then, 'My second, northern Egypt and the Suez Canal.'

Rommel was absolutely convinced by mobile operations, and believed in leading his Panzer force from the front, or as he himself said, 'from the saddle'. Out in the desert Rommel was to be found again and again with the leading tank, the leading platoon or seen with the leading company commander. As a commander Rommel was not a very easy general to serve. Like so many German commanders he could only command in his own way, in the way he had learned in the trenches of the First World War, and then in France twenty-two years later. But the impact on the battlefield had undoubtedly printed an unforgettable image on the mind of every soldier in his command. For these young men fighting in the desert under Rommel were quickly able to generate the sense of belonging and 'unit pride', which was an essential ingredient to any combat formation that had to battle across such inhospitable terrain.

By early March 1941 Rommel had unleashed his Afrika-Korps against the British. Within a month Rommel's force had left a trail of destruction leading to the smouldering town of Benghazi. In a letter home, Rommel wrote to his wife boasting about his one-main desert Blitzkrieg, and his almost total disobedience: 'My superiors in Tripoli, Rome and perhaps Berlin must be holding their heads in dismay. I took the risk, against all orders and instructions, because the opportunity was there…'

In Berlin news of Rommel's personal exploits across the desert were met with dismay. Although Hitler was pleased with his over-ambitious general, he instructed him by radio to halt. But once again Rommel, master of deception, ignored the German High Command, telling the Italian commander Gariboldi that he had just been given complete freedom of action across the desert.

On 4 April, under the shimmering high-noon sun, Rommel's mixed force began their assault across the desert. The high daytime temperatures, and the sand sifting through into the vehicles' engines, soon brought many vehicles to a grinding halt. In order to keep his struggling columns moving, Rommel took personal command and decided to direct movements from the air, or from his small fighting command group of three vehicles. On occasion from his Storch he would fly in low and drop a message on a column: 'If you don't move off again at once, I'll come down – Rommel!' To him speed was all that mattered now. Continuously he hunted for a column, which had taken too long or had mistaken its direction. With his sudden presence and his sharp tongue, he goaded, improvised and galvanized every part of his command. In front of his startled and fumbling enemy he had shown total dominance and a firm attitude in his disregard of danger. Remorselessly he pushed his men to breaking point, but they knew that with competent leadership they could win. For the next few months that followed, Rommels superior tactics, coupled with the stubborn resistance of German and Italian troops, brought a string of victories. At home his reputation grew to new heights with Reich radios blaring out waves of exaltation for their 'Desert Fox'. His victorious Cyrenaican campaign, which had forced some of the most irrepressible Empire troops to withdraw in their thousands across the desert, was soon known around the world. Intoxicated by these spectacular victories, he began dreaming of soon conquering North Africa. Even as the first reports of Germany's invasion of Russia reached Rommel, he began to investigate ways of capturing the heavily defended garrison of Tobruk first, then, striking-out across the frontier wire into Egypt from the west, while the German Army, after capturing the Caucasus, would come down and invade Egypt from the east. However, the British were more determined than ever to prevent Rommel's Afrika-Korps from invading Egypt and reaching the Nile.

For the next year in the desert, Rommel continued to display a dogged effort in trying to smash the British forces. Again and again he showed all the hallmarks of a great commander by constantly outwitting, outmanoeuvring and outgunning his bewildered enemy. Whenever there was a problem on the battlefield he was often seen frantically bucketing through the desert in his vehicle, screaming out orders to prevent a rout and keep his forces moving. He hardly allowed his exhausted men to pause and this in turn brought a number of well-earned victories for him. Despite the overwhelming odds Rommel went on to outmanoeuvre and outfight the Allies, and nearly destroyed the British 8th Army. In June 1942 he pursued his defeated enemies to Tobruk, which he finally captured on 21 June. The next day, from Hitler's East Prussian headquarters, an exalted Führer promoted Rommel to Field Marshal.

At only fifty-years old Rommel was the youngest Field Marshal in the German Army. He celebrated by drinking a glass of captured whisky and a tin of pineapple. Rommel wrote to his wife that night: 'Hitler has made me a Field Marshal. I would, however, have preferred to have been given one more division.'

With the air of a victorious warlord, Rommel now ventured into unknown terrain, leading his troops in broad formation against the well-defended town of El Alamein. Throughout July and early August, the Desert Fox pounded away at the El Alamein position, but the 8th Army repeatedly thwarted Rommel's attempts to crush their strong defences. In spite of determined attacks by the Afrika-Korps, the troops were wearing under the strain and his health also was suffering. The harsh environment of the North African desert had made Rommel sick and exhausted. Suffering from desert sores, circulatory problems, chronic stomach and intestinal problems as well as liver trouble, he left North Africa for recuperation in a mountain resort near Vienna.

When Rommel returned to North Africa in late October the situation in the desert was dire. But once again undeterred and resilient as ever, he did a magnificent job holding British forces for more than a week at El Alamein. However, by November he admitted defeat and ordered a general retreat of his forces.

El Alamein was a turning point for the North Afrika-Korps, including Rommel's relationship with Hitler. After the demise of operations in North Africa the Desert Fox was treated like other top ranking Generals visiting the Führer headquarters. During Hitler's lengthy conferences Rommel had to listen to charges of defeatism and other forms of unreasonable and irrational behaviour. During one military conference Hitler even questioned the courage of the Afrika-Korps, whereupon Rommel walked out of the room.

Out in North Africa, with nothing but a string of defeats since El Alamein, Rommel conducted a brilliant one thousand mile retreat and got the remnants of his Afrika-Korps to Tunisia in early 1943. Throughout the Africa campaign Rommel had been a leading spirit. His speed of perception, energy and boldness of concept had placed him as one of the greatest commanders in history. He was not only shrewd and a practical man but was a realist as well. From the start he had dominated the battlefield. He had been bold in attack, ferocious in pursuit of the enemy, and obsessed with obtaining his objective, but by March 1943 he had finally met his match. The threat of the 'Desert Fox' in Africa had once and for all finally been vanquished.

A photograph taken of Rommel's Tripoli headquarters in 1941. General Rommel wasted no time after his arrival at his headquarters to start planning for the first Afrika-Korps attacks against the British.

General Rommel was one of the greatest military tacticians of all time. Here in this photograph he is seen planning, with the aid of a large map, the first attacks against British positions.

A member of the headquarters staff is making final corrections to Rommel's plans prior to the Afrika-Korps unleashing its might in the desert. Rommel's objective was to be the re-conquest of Cyrenaica.

General Rommel discusses his battle plans with an Italian general whilst walking along a road in the centre of Tripoli in February 1941. When Rommel arrived in Tripoli the Italian Army was close to collapse. The General immediately visited the Italian commander General Gariboldi to discuss the dire situation in Libya.

Two photographs taken in sequence showing General Rommel seen conferring with officers, probably after a military parade in Tripoli in February 1941. During the initial stages of the German build-up Rommel exaggerated the Afrika-Korps' strength by sending his armour around the block several times. Deception and bluff were to become the hallmarks of Rommel's campaign in North Africa.

Rommel is seen conferring with an Italian general in Tripoli in February 1941. Rommel was eventually to have little time for Italian senior officers, but had a paternal way with their soldiers. Although there were the obvious language problems, Rommel's drive and energy helped turn around the Italian army's low morale.

Inside an aircraft hanger Rommel is speaking to Italian officers. In front of them is a Fieseler Storch reconnaissance and communications aircraft. The Fieseler Storch was used extensively in North Africa and Rommel himself actually used one in order to direct movements of his armour from the air.

A Fieseler Storch preparing to depart and take to the skies. The Fieseler Storch, for its size and weight, was a very versatile, sturdy and robust aircraft. They were a common feature in the skies about Libya in 1941 and 1942. In fact, they were so popular that one captured Storch became the personal aircraft of Field Marshal Montgomery.

Rommel confers with two German officers whilst strolling along a cobbled street in Tripoli in February or March 1941. Although Rommel knew his Afrika-Korps were outnumbered against the British, he had ambitious plans for his men.

Three photographs showing General Rommel flanked by German officers speaking with Italian commanders. When Rommel arrived in North Africa his mission was ostensibly to explore the military situation, but he knew it would be his force that would prevent the advance of the British through Libya, and not the Italians.

Five photographs showing Rommel in his command car during the African campaign between 1941 and 1942. Rommel was often seen standing in his command car; his constant presence on the front line was an inspiration to his men and the key to his leadership. He was a commander that preferred to sit in the front of his car with his driver, rather than sit in the back. From this vantage point, he could survey the landscape as he passed through and be able to quickly direct his forces from one position to another. By travelling through the desert in his car, instead of remaining at his headquarters in Tripoli, he was not only able to see for himself first hand the battles that raged in the desert, but was able to generate morale and fighting spirit among his men.

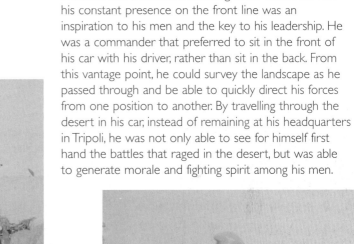

From an observation post Rommel, accompanied by two members of staff, observes enemy movement in the distance. Rommel believed in leading his force from the front and it was for this reason his men constantly found him with the leading platoon or leading company commander.

Throughout the North African campaign Rommel displayed great determination and dogged effort by outwitting, outmanoeuvring, and outgunning his enemy. Even during the last months of the campaign, he maximized the disadvantages of his dwindling force, which led to a number of small-scale battles being won.

Rommel, flanked by officers, strolls through the desert. As a commander Rommel was unanimously appreciated and admired by both friends and foe alike. Out in the field he tried to suffer every hardship his men suffered. He even tried to live under the same conditions as his men.

Rommel conferring with his officers. Undoubtedly Rommel's iron will as commander drove his Afrika-Korps on relentlessly and made sure his presence in the front line was known, whether he was travelling in his command vehicle or flying above them in his Storch aircraft.

Rommel is pictured here conferring with Italian officers on the next strategic move in the desert. Prior to Rommel's arrival in North Africa, the Italian Army had been humiliated by a string of defeats. Now under his command both the Afrika-Korps and Italian Army would successfully strike out across Libya and score sizable victories.

One of Rommel's officers survey the battlefield through a pair of binoculars. Constantly the 'Desert Fox' would travel across the desert trying to formulate a masterstroke against his Allied foes.

An interesting photograph taken of Rommel standing next to his Horch field staff car with German and Italian officers. Rommel was without a doubt a master tactician. His officers and personal staff soon recognised a commanding intelligence of rare capacity.

Pictured with Italian and German officers, Rommel confers about the progress on the battlefield. Although Rommel's tactical plans were sometimes over-ambitious, his Blitzkrieg campaign through the desert was supported by the authorities in both Rome and Berlin.

Two photographs taken in sequence and showing Rommel pictured wearing a life jacket preparing to fly back to Italy in a Heinkel. Being away from the front on trips to Italy and Germany made Rommel anxious. He constantly worried that, without his competent leadership, there would a reversal of fortune in the desert.

Rommel conferring with his men whilst seated inside his Horch field staff car during operations at El Alamein in August 1942. From his staff car Rommel actually watched the battle unfold. It was a critical element in the campaign in North Africa.

Two photographs taken in sequence showing Rommel strolling with one of his commanding officers out in the desert. The Afrika-Korps had meanwhile implemented Rommel's tactics using quick, decisive lightening attacks and penetrating into the enemy's main arteries.

A rare moment for the 'Desert Fox' pictured here relaxing in an Italian deckchair. Two of the officers with him can be seen using jerry cans as seating. Note how the bleaching effects from the heat of the sun and desert air have given their tunics a dirty appearance.

Rommel can be seen directing the movements of his force prior to an attack. Before any attack Rommel made sure that everything was in order. After extensive reconnaissance patrols using small detachments of infantry and tanks, anti-tank guns and tanks, supported by motorized infantry, were brought up within striking distance of the enemy. When the attack was finally unleashed tanks would move forward first, supported by heavy fire from artillery.

Two photographs taken in sequence showing Rommel with the aid of a map scrutinizing the next strategic move in the desert with his staff officers. Rommel was totally aware that he was fighting an enemy that were far superior to him in numbers, so nothing in the planning was left to chance. Behind Rommel and his three commanders is a curious crewmember of a Pz.Kpfw.III, who can be seen peering through the one-piece entry hatch on the side of the turret.

Two photographs showing Rommel with his officers conferring about the next planned move on the battlefield. Throughout the campaign in North Africa Rommel fought a chivalrous warfare. Unlike the brutal fighting that raged on the Eastern Front, he had ordered his men to fight cleanly and respect the enemy. So powerful was Rommel's myth as a great commander, it even captivated Montgomery himself.

Rommel standing in front of his forward command post whilst one of his aids can be seen clutching a piece of paper behind him. In spite of the success Rommel gained in North Africa, by 1942 the harsh environment in the desert had made him a sick man.

Chapter Three

Desert War Unleashed 1941

In March 1941 Rommel's information about the strength of the British was still incomplete. But what was certain in his intelligence report was that the port of Tobruk was full of shipping, and there appeared to be large movements of troops concentrating around the harbour. Unknown to Rommel or his staff the British were in fact not bringing in reinforcements by sea, but were withdrawing the bulk of their best units from Libya to launch a military operation in Greece. By the time the British were aware that Hitler had sent an expeditionary force to North Africa, it was too late. Rommel had already ordered General Johannes Streich to drive eastwards along the coast from Syrte with advanced units of the 5th Light Division. By 4 March Streich had successfully reached Mugtaa, which was a strong point, difficult for the enemy to attack. But still there was no contact with British forces. In a letter Rommel wrote optimistically of their advance: 'the front is now 480 miles east [of Tripoli]…my soldiers are being moved over. It's tempo that matters now.' Rommel was now in sight of his re-conquest of Cyrenaica and was sure that the brunt of the fighting would come there.

Days later, when Rommel arrived back from Berlin after receiving the Oakleaves to his Knight's Cross, he found more evidence of British troops still in retreat. At Mugtaa Streich's light forces suddenly confronted enemy soldiers and quickly and decisively drove them from their meagre defences with hardly a fight. With nothing to stop Streich's men they chased the British across the desert towards the little town of Mersa el Brega. While British forces begun frantically digging in and bringing up additional reinforcements around the town, Streich was ordered by Rommel to attack enemy positions, regardless of the Berlin directive which stipulated that Rommel was not to attack Mersa el Brega until the end of May. As predicted, like at Mugtaa, the British abandoned their positions and Rommel, now brimming with confidence, ordered that the entire area facing the east was to be laid with a strong belt of mines and anti-aircraft guns to prevent the enemy from returning.

By early April Rommel realized that the British were now desperately trying to keep their forces together and had begun a painful retreat from the peninsula of Cyrenaica. Still unwilling to allow the enemy time to regroup and bring up more armour, Rommel continued disobeying orders and instructed a dramatic three pronged all-out assault, determined to exploit their enemy. German units, backed by Italian divisions, attacked the British defenders and dislodged them from what would have become an excellent defensive position. In the aftermath that followed, they laid a trail of destruction to the town of Benghazi.

Now with a string of victories, the Afrika-Korps continued exploiting the desert of North Africa by pushing further east and driving the British back. After a nearly 220-mile march across the desert, Tobruk was now with in their grasp.

Rommel was totally aware of the significance of capturing Tobruk and he knew this had to be undertaken before he resumed his eastward drive towards Egypt. Tobruk was regarded as the most important port in North Africa and was occupied by the British. Sitting in his Italian-built caravan trailer, which was moved just south of the Tobruk front line, Rommel spent many hours preparing the assault on the town. He was convinced that the British were pulling out and retreating into the port to stage a second Dunkirk style evacuation. But unknown to Rommel, Winston Churchill had already ordered that the port be held to the death without retirement. This was not going to be another Dunkirk. Instead, it was going to be the longest siege in British military history.

On 11 April, the first series of attacks were unleashed by the Afrika-Korps against the heavily defended Tobruk garrison, which consisted of both British and Commonwealth troops. Six German artillery battalions, including an Italian artillery regiment and a flak battery for close support, poured a concentrated storm of shell fire onto the enemy, and sappers were moved forward to blow in the tank ditches. But time and time again the fortress of Tobruk stubbornly resisted.

For the next weeks and months to come, bloody and violent German ground and aerial bombardments tried to smash the resistance at Tobruk. Late that summer, whilst the fighting continued around the port, the Afrika-Korps were strengthened and upgraded to Panzergruppe Afrika or Panzer Group Africa. It now boasted six Italian divisions and included the Afrika-Korps, comprising the 15th and 21st Panzer Divisions, and the 90th Light Division, which included old units of the 5th Light Division. Troop strength now numbered some 55,000 men.

Whilst the Afrika-Korps were being bolstered with additional forces, Britain too reinforced her army, re-organizing the Western Desert Force to the British 8th Army. In front of Rommel they prepared to launch a massive offensive to destroy him before he could knock out the Tobruk garrison. By November 1941 British reinforcements were assembled and ready for the attack. For nearly three days 100,000 British troops and more than 700 tanks were poised in the baking sun ready to spring their attack on the Afrika-Korps. On 18 November the stillness of the desert was suddenly shattered by the sounds of heavy gunfire as the British offensive finally began with a series of savage tank battles. Across an area of about fifty square miles in the west, tanks duelled tanks. Soon the battlefield was littered with the dead and burnt-out hulks of armoured vehicles. Although the Afrika-Korps were outnumbered against excellently armed and equipped soldiers, they were still as determined as ever to prevent the British hammering a corridor through to Tobruk. With staggering losses they managed to blunt the British offensive and even set out, against Hitler's direction, to crush the British 7th Armoured Division.

By late November British lines once again stiffened and with further reinforcements they now began streaming towards Rommel's exhausted and badly depleted positions. With no fuel, ammunition or reserves left to sustain them in battle, he ordered a general retreat from Cyrenaica including dismantling his siege apparatus around Tobruk. For the first time in Rommel's life he was on the retreat. On Christmas day Benghazi was left to fall into British hands and by the end of 1941 Rommel was back where he had begun the previous spring.

Despite Rommel's retreat across nearly 300 miles of desert, his force had in fact withdrawn without serious loss, and were still able to inflict terrible wounds on the enemy. Undeterred as ever, Rommel was still determined to launch a new offensive. First he was going to re-supply, rehabilitate and reorganize his forces, and he also planned to lay 100,000 mines in a new line, which he said would be a kind of East Wall to protect Tripolitania.

A poster depicting two Afrika-Korps soldiers wearing the pith helmet and familiar tropical uniform during the onset of the campaign in Libya in 1941. Much was made of the campaign in Africa, with the Nazi government determined to bring about a sense of camaraderie in the desert.

Here forces from the new Afrika-Korps charged through British defensive positions near Mugtaa in early March 1941. By 4 March advanced units from General Streich`s 5th Light Division had reached Mugtaa where it later clashed with enemy forces. Within days the Afrika-Korps were driving the British back across the desert.

A German soldier or engineer appears to be unearthing one of the many thousands of mines laid in the desert. Minefields were a constant problem for both sides and could effectively hold up entire divisions, or even armies, for days whilst a path was cleared.

What appears to be one of the very few Pz.Kpfw.IIIs moving across the desert, whilst in action during the initial stages of the campaign in March or April 1941. The British were completely surprised by the German attack and were compelled to begin what they saw as a bitter and bloody retreat through Cyrenaica.

Officers can be seen conferring with each other whilst standing next to a mobile field kitchen. Four of the men are wearing the enlisted men's field caps.

Both German and Italian soldiers gather around an artillery gun during the primary stages of the campaign during March or April 1941. A number of soldiers are wearing the pith helmet with their standard tropical uniform. These conventional sun helmets were widely issued to troops in 1941. Although not very popular among the soldiers, who almost invariably discarded it in favour of the field cap, the pith helmet continued to be worn, often behind front lines, for semi-formal occasions, including parades and ceremonies.

Out in the desert German and Italian officers discuss the war situation in April 1941. By this period the Afrika-Korps, with Italian forces, were exploiting the desert and pushing further east, driving the British back.

German troops advance slowly across the desert supported by a Pz.Kpfw.III. In the distance other vehicles can be seen, purposely spaced out in order to minimise the risk of an aerial attack.

A British defensive position has been occupied by Afrika-Korps troops during its furious drive across Cyrenaica. The objective of the Germans was to eliminate as many enemy defensive positions as possible and force their way forward rapidly, trying to incur minimal numbers of casualties.

Vehicles from Rommel's mixed force move across the desert of Cyrenaica. The Germans made full use of the freedom of manoeuvre, which the desert terrain offered. However, the harsh environment caused many vehicles to overheat or develop more serious mechanical problems. With supplies sometimes stretched to capacity, vehicles regularly became stranded for hours, with crews either burning in the sun or freezing in the dark.

Afrika-Korps troops crossing a battlefield during the initial push for Tobruk in April 1941. The soldiers are all distinctively wearing their sand-camouflaged M1935 steel helmets under battle conditions. In the foreground at least two of the soldiers are armed with MG34 machine guns, which are slung over their shoulders for ease of carriage.

Afrika-Korps troops on board a halftrack Sd.Kfz.251, which is armed with two MG34 machine guns for local defence. The Sd.Kfz.251 performed very well in the extreme conditions encountered in the desert and was used extensively by the Germans to move troops from one battle front to another.

Plumes of smoke rise skyward during intensive German attacks against British and Commonwealth positions during the early stages of the battle for Tobruk. The battle of Tobruk became the longest siege in British military history and one of the bloodiest and most violent battles to rage in all of the Western Desert campaigns.

Afrika-Korps troops digging in around Tobruk in April/May 1941. A 3.7cm Pak 35/36 anti-tank gun can be seen in a well-concealed position. One of the gunners can just be seen with his gun hidden behind the sandbags.

Panzers belonging to the 5th Light Division move through the desert bound for positions around Tobruk in April 1941. For the next weeks and months to come, bloody and violent German ground and aerial attacks were unleashed against British and Commonwealth forces. Rommel himself became obsessed with destroying the garrison and capturing the port.

A tent has been erected near Tobruk in May 1941. Sandbags were often placed around or beneath the tent to absorb sandstorms. Sand-filled tins and boxes enabled the soldier to sleep without the prospect of his tent being blown.

A flak observation unit survey the sky for enemy aircraft. The RAF often hindered German operations in the Western Desert and as a consequence anti-aircraft guns were exployed to deal with the growing threat.

Conditions out in the desert were often very difficult for the soldier. Personal hygiene also posed its own problems. Here in this photograph is an off-duty soldier combing his hair with the aid of a shaving mirror. Note the bare minimum of clothing worn.

Soldiers confer with each other at a field post near Tobruk in 1941. Rommel had made it clear to his commanding officers that before the Afrika-Korps could wage an offensive against Egypt, the capture of Tobruk must be the first objective. For this prime reason the 'Desert Fox' urged the German High Command to send additional forces and supplies needed for the attack against the well-defended garrison at Tobruk.

Afrika-Korps commanders confer with Italian officers. Between April and June 1941 the Afrika-Korps lacked communications and reinforcements. The Italian force too was badly equipped and could barely support Rommel's drive through the desert.

Afrika-Korps commanders discuss the military situation with the aid of maps on a clipboard. When the Afrika-Korps initially attacked through the desert the Italian commanders had difficulty accepting Rommel's tactics of rapid desert warfare.

During a lull in the advance, troops have time to relax and can be seen in the desert having fun. Life in the desert was often very hard and conditions were invariably difficult for the men.

Afrika-Korps commanders are seen conferring and watch armoured vehicles moving through the desert. This photograph was taken in June 1941. It was during this period when the Commonwealth's 'Western Desert Force' was renamed the 8th Army with General Cunningham as its commander.

Here Afrika-Korps troops can be seen unloading large drums of fuel from a captured British supply train. For both sides, supplying their forces in the vast sprawling desert of North Africa was vital for the continuation of the war.

Under the baking hot sun a photograph shows a group of Afrika-Korps officers with their commander. The majority of the men are wearing the tropical service tunic and field cap headgear.

An officer wearing a motorcyclist greatcoat is seen holding a turtle, much to the enjoyment of his fellow officers.

Here a German soldier takes a photograph of a sign erected by the British, naming the route after the British commander General Wavell, and altering it to 'Rommel Way'.

It was between May and June 1941 that General Wavell had attacked the Halfaya-Capuzzo line to reduce Axis pressure on Tobruk, known as 'operation Battleaxe'. However, Wavell did not have the military genius of Rommel and his forces were soon pushed back.

Two soldiers can be seen standing next to a Pz.Kpfw.III. In the Afrika-Korps each tank regiment contained some 204 Panzers, of which 136 were light armoured combat vehicles or Panzers, consisting of Pz.Kpfw.Is and IIs, and only 68 medium and heavy Pz.Kpfw.III and IVs.

Two photographs showing the same flak gun attached on the rear of a truck. Both the 2cm and 3.7cm flak gun were very effective weapons and were used both against ground and aerial targets. Note smoke rising in the distance, indicating that a heavy calibre shell has probably hit a target in the village.

German armoured vehicles moving through the desert using the famous Afrika-Korps 'V' formation. This type of armoured formation was used extensively in the desert. Typically a battalion of tanks consisting of around 75 Panzers used this formation, with two companies leading and one in reserve.

A Pz.Kpfw.III ploughs through the desert, its tracks churning up huge amounts of dust. Vehicles moving through the desert were often easy targets as the dust could be seen from many miles away.

A Pz.Kpfw.III climbs a steep gradient and is carefully directed by one of the crew members who can be seen in front of the vehicle. The tank has a host of provisions on board and attached to the turret side are stick grenades for local defence.

Pz.Kpfw.IIIs move forward in the desert. Between February and April 1941 the Afrika-Korps consisted of the 5th Panzer Regiment and later the 15th Panzer Division, which was composed of the 8th Panzer Regiment. Rommel's Panzers moved through the desert in dramatic exploits, reminiscent of the Blitzkrieg campaigns fought in 1939 and 1940.

Vehicles of the 15th Panzer Division move along a road. The division consisted of the 8th Panzer Regiment, 15th Rifle Brigade, 33rd Artillery Regiment, 33rd Reconnaissance Battalion, 33rd Panzerjager Battalion and the 33rd Pioneer Battalion.

A signals engineer can be seen setting up an overhead telephone line. Initially when the Afrika-Korps arrived, virtually all lines were installed along the ground, but because of the vast amounts of traffic passing over them the Germans were soon compelled to erect them overhead to avoid the lines becoming damaged or severed.

Four photographs showing Field Marshal Kesselring's arrival in North Africa. His visit was not only to oversee personally Luftwaffe operations in North Africa, but also to inspire courage and determination into his Luftwaffe crews. Field Marshal Kesselring was the senior officer of all the German troops in the Mediterranean. He had no direct operational command at this time, but was responsible for the assembly in Italy of all German supplies for the forces in North Africa. Kesselring's stay in North Africa was often marred by rows with Rommel. Even up to the time Kesselring left Africa, Rommel did not think very highly of him. During the course of the war though, his opinion was later to change.

An 8.8cm flak gun being readied for action in a ground role. Note the close proximity of the flak gun's limber. When the 8.8cm gun was in action the limber was normally found positioned very near, just in case the crew needed to hastily move the weapon to another position. Sometimes the gun was used in action on the limber but the instability affected accuracy and the rate of fire.

German and Italian soldiers pose for the camera with a stationary tank. Out in the desert the Afrika Korps initially relied quite heavily on the lighter tanks to provide the armoured punch. Consequently this put increasing strain on the light tanks and caused a high percentage of mechanical problems.

Herman Goring, commander of the Luftwaffe, inspects Luftwaffe crews in Italy prior to their deployment to North Africa. Although the fighting in Africa was primarily a land role, the Luftwaffe played an essential supporting part in the successes of Rommel's forces in North Africa.

Pz.Kpfw.II's roll along a road towards the front lines in the summer of 1941. Although these vehicles were under-gunned and under-armoured they still managed to fight with relative success on the battlefield. However, by late the following year, the majority of the Pz.Kpfw.IIs were withdrawn from the front and performed scouting missions instead.

A grenadier is about to throw a stick grenade from his slit trench during the battle of Tobruk. Initially Rommel's attack against the strongly held garrison at Tobruk had little effect. In spite of his failure to smash through the defensive positions, the Afrika Korps did manage to drive the British out of Cyrenaica in less than two weeks.

Afrika Korps troops wearing Pith helmets rest out in the desert with their Pak 35/36 anti-tank gun. Canvas sheeting is partially covering the weapon, not only to protect it from the harsh environment, but also to camouflage the gun from the enemy.

A truck more than likely laden with supplies has halted on a road. The vehicle can clearly be seen with an application of yellow-brown paint. Although the vehicles were often well camouflaged by the end of 1941, the harsh environment soon bleached, peeled and sanded off the paint.

A soldier wearing a pith helmet is typing a report. In the heat troops often discarded their uniforms in order to try and remain as cool as possible.

As Rommel's forces struck through Cyrenaica British forces were driven hastily from their positions. The speed of the Afrika-Korps often led to enemy troops reluctantly abandoning their equipment. Here in this photograph is an abandoned British 25-pounder, which was more than capable of knocking out light and medium tanks.

An officer surveys the terrain using a pair of scissor binoculars. Using scissor binoculars the officer can calculate the range of a target and these were specifically designed to observe over a parapet of a trench unhindered by the enemy.

A flak crew with their 2cm flak gun are watched by intrigued locals. As with all other theatres of war, the German anti-aircraft artillery or flak guns were primarily used to defend a position against attacking aircraft.

Two photographs showing two captured Matilda tanks. During 1941 and early 1942 the Matilda proved to be a highly effective vehicle against both German and Italian tanks, although it was very vulnerable against the larger calibre anti-tank guns like the 8.8cm.

Smiling for the camera is a group of captured British soldiers. Unlike the war being raged that year on the Eastern Front in Russia, the desert war was generally regarded as a 'gentlemanly' war, with both sides treating their prisoners well.

Near to the coast of Benghazi captured British troops are waiting to be shipped back to mainland Europe in order to minimise the drain on the Afrika Korps supplies.

After unloading their 8.8cm flak gun from the limber, the crew hastily prepare their weapon for action deep in the desert. In the distance a halftrack can be seen, which probably had another 8.8cm flak gun on tow. Preparing artillery and flak guns for action on the battlefield relied heavily on the various light and heavy armoured vehicles for transportation. Maintaining the momentum of the advance in the desert was vital to success, and without transport, the whole advance might stall.

A Pak gun, well concealed beneath camouflage netting, trains its powerful gun barrel from a position overlooking the sea. Like the vehicles' artillery, flak and Pak guns all received a liberal application of dull yellow sand-coloured paint. Covered with a camouflage net and hidden among rocks the gun blended well onto the sandy terrain.

Here Zeltbahn tents give additional shelter to troops. Tents were the most common feature of desert living in North Africa. They were not only very practical but easily erected. As with the majority of tents erected a trench was dug first, which was deep and wide enough to take the tent and allow the soldier room for manoeuvre whilst sheltering inside.

Out in the desert troops have erected at least three tents all in close proximity of each other. In order to reduce the possibility of the tents being blown away in the often-strong sandstorms, rocks have been constructed around the tents.

A variety of vehicles were pressed into service in North Africa. The distances which the Afrika Korps had to travel were vast and a multitude of captured vehicles were utilised to cope with the harsh climate and terrain. In this photograph Afrika Korps soldiers examine captured British vehicles including a Morris C8 4 x 4 'Quad' field artillery tractor, which was used for towing field guns and ammunition limbers.

A 15cm howitzer being readied for action. The canvas sheeting will be pulled off and the camouflage netting, which can be seen heaped over the trail spades, will be placed over the entire gun. Apart from concealing the weapon, camouflage nets also served to deny the enemy the ability to identify the type of artillery piece that occupied the position.

Positioned inside a freshly dug pit is a Luftwaffe 3.7cm flak gun crew. The crew have elevated the barrel in preparation against aerial targets detected in the vicinity. Note the kill rings painted either in yellow or white on the gun barrel.

A group of Pz.Kpfw.IV tanks move forward into action. The Panzer IV was regarded as the workhorse of the German tank corps, and consequently saw action in all theatres of combat throughout the war, including North Africa.

An 8.8cm flak gun being fired against a ground target from its limber. Out on the battlefield the 8.8cm proved a very versatile weapon and continued being used in a duel anti-tank and anti-aircraft role throughout the campaign in North Africa.

Members of a Luftwaffe ground crew stand to attention next to their Messerschmitt Me 109 during a visit by Field Marshal Kesselring. German fighter aircraft played a prominent role in Rommel's advance through the desert and were able not only to attack and destroy enemy aircraft, but to hinder enemy troop concentrations, in order to allow the Afrika Korps to further exploit the desert towards the Egyptian frontier.

British PoWs pose for the camera after being captured in late 1941. Whilst in captivity in North Africa the PoWs were relatively well kept and given basic rations.

In what appears to be a press photograph, a soldier wearing the famous pith helmet points to the port of Tripoli on a map. Throughout 1941 thousands of tons of supplies poured through the port, ensuring that the Afrika Korps retained its fighting position in North Africa.

Two Afrika Korps soldiers pose for the camera with a captured battle flag of the British 259th Battery, Norfolk Yeomanry Regiment.

Pz.Kpfw.35 (t)s can be seen in the desert in 1941. Note the turret hatches are open in a drastic attempt by the crew to cool the inside of the tank. However, for safety's sake hatches were normally closed down if the enemy was in close proximity. The crew would then have to endure sweating and choking, sometimes for hours for the vehicles' air filters would often become clogged as they crossed the dusty and sandy terrain.

A well-positioned 8.8cm flak gun can be seen in its full-elevated position poised for action against enemy aircraft. The barrel of the gun has victory markings painted either in yellow or white. These were known as barrel kill rings and German military units painted them on their guns or vehicles that had destroyed enemy aircraft, vehicles, or other targets. This particular flak gun has been painted with three kill rings.

Chapter Four

Year of Decision 1942

During the first weeks of January 1942 Rommel tirelessly inspected his units digging in along the line at Mersa El Brega. For days he brooded over maps, photographs and intelligence reports, preparing his Panzer group not for defence, but for a surprise attack against the British. On 21 January his surprise attack began in earnest. Almost immediately the Afrika-Korps outwitted, outmanoeuvred and outgunned its bewildered enemy. Within five days the Germans had knocked out and captured 299 enemy tanks and armoured fighting vehicles, 147 guns and taken 935 prisoners. The British were now in full retreat, and the smouldering town of Benghazi once again changed hands. In just two weeks the Afrika-Korps had bulldozed half way back across Cyrenaica, and for this triumphant military feat Hitler promoted Rommel to Colonel General. With Hitler's faith now restored, Rommel was determined to re- conquer all Cyrenaica, capture Tobruk, and advance with all his might on Egypt and the Nile.

In April, after a lull in fighting, Rommel secretly reshuffled his Panzer army to prepare them for an attack on the British Gazala line that ran down from the defence line, which already boasted half a million mines. Rommel chose a daring plan by sending his entire tank strength on an outflanking move round the southern end of the Gazala line in an attempt to dupe the enemy. Then he planned to drive north and capture Tobruk. The plan was so bold Rommel knew if he lost this battle, he stood to lose all Africa.

On 26 May 1942, the attack finally began with Rommel's entire striking force of over 10,000 vehicles moving south against the setting sun. What followed was complete chaos as enemy tanks suddenly ripped through the German right flank. By the following day almost one-third of the Afrika-Korps armour was lost. A few days later wild rumours spread that the British had encircled the Afrika-Korps and that Rommel was dead. But a few days later Rommel established radio contact with his headquarters. There now seemed a glimmer of hope, despite the increasing casualty rate. Still undaunted by his formidable enemy, Rommel attacked the strongpoint at Got el Oualeb, while the Italians charged from the west. By 2 June he had a victory. The British 150th Infantry Brigade and 1st Army Tank Brigade surrendered and 3,000 soldiers, 124 guns and 101 armoured vehicles of all descriptions were captured. Now Rommel, exhausted by battle and sweltering heat, pushed his forces through the minefield and closed in around the heavily defended town of Bir Hakeim. For eight days, completely surrounded, the 1st Free French Brigade held out valiantly until they finally capitulated. The British 8th Army, now in danger of being encircled, attempted to fall back towards Tobruk. What was left in its wake was nothing but destroyed tanks, empty, burnt and blasted slit trenches and the scattered belongings of the dead.

Rommel was now free to wheel northward through the disintegrating Gazala line and moved forward with twice the number of tanks of the British. His path was now wrenched wide-open leading to Tobruk.

On 18 June Rommel moved in to take his prize. While his forces massed outside the perimeter and surrounded the port, Stukas pounded it mercilessly. With every punishing attack the dive-bombers peeled off and screamed down on their targets. Then, as the aerial bombardment subsided, the Afrika-Korps and the 20th Italian Corps bombarded the town with literally hundreds of artillery pieces. By 21 June Tobruk finally surrendered. 'Today', 'Rommel said in a German radio announcement, 'my troops have crowned their efforts by the capture of Tobruk.'

After the victorious announcement of the capitulation of Tobruk the Afrika-Korps pushed eastwards. By early July they were now only 100 miles from the great British Naval base at Alexandria. In Cairo, a state of emergency had been declared. The objective was now Egypt. In broad formation the Afrika-Korps drove further than it had ever advanced before, venturing into unknown terrain. However, between the advancing German forces and Egypt stood the well-fortified town of El Alamein.

Throughout July and the first half of August the Afrika-Korps pounded away at El Alamein, but the 8th Army repeatedly thwarted Rommel's fierce attempts to crush their strong consolidation. After seventeen months of battling across the desert, his army was wearing under the strain, and so was his health. He was 16,000 men below strength, and sickness was reaching epidemic proportions. For the attack against El Alamein Rommel could only field some 203 Panzers against 767 of Field Marshal Montgomery's. Yet, in spite the drying up of supplies and the overwhelming numbers of the British, Rommel still prepared his men on 30 August for one last attempt to smash through enemy positions and charge into the heart of Egypt.

All along the German front the Afrika-Korps, with all its remaining armour, finally began its long awaited attack and pushed out eastward through thousands of mines defended stubbornly by infantry equipped with artillery, guns, and mortars. Almost immediately the Afrika-Korps came up against stiff resistance and brought leading elements of the advance to an abrupt halt. Bitter fighting engulfed the area and during the bloody battle that ensued, Lieutenant General Nehring of the 15th Panzer Division was severely injured by air attack, and Major General von Bismarck of the 21st Panzer Division killed by a mine.

For the next few weeks the battle raged, as the British finally brought the climactic showdown at El Alamein to a head by the third week of October 1942. British forces surged forward in a series of ferocious attacks and pounded the Afrika-Korps, causing many losses. By 25 October both armies had been fighting continuously without respite. But the Allies, now taking advantage of the German losses, continued advancing through the minefield in the west and even managed to wrench open a five-mile deep gap. British troops quickly took up positions atop the Miteriya Ridge in the southeast, but both the Afrika-Korps and Italian forces were still firmly entrenched in most of their original positions. With the battle now almost fought to a standstill, the British evacuated the Miteriya Ridge and swung northwards toward the sea. The battle would now be concentrated in the area around Tel al-Eissa until they were able to make a breakthrough.

For the next seven days fighting was fierce as the Germans tried in vain to capture the high ground around Tel al-Eissa, which was so vital to their defence. Rommel was so determined to take the high ground that he instructed both the 21st Panzer Division and Ariete Armoured Division to help smash the British and Commonwealth positions. However, due the lack of fuel the vehicles could not retire from the battlefield and were stuck on open ground and attacked by British aircraft.

Fighting in the area continued to rage but by the end of October the German losses and the lack of supplies were seriously impeding operations. Reluctantly, Rommel planned a general withdrawal of his forces towards Fuka, a few miles west. By early November, Rommel had lost nearly 12,000 men and 350 Panzers. Only a handful of tanks were now at his disposal. With his forces now fighting for survival the 'Desert Fox' sent an urgent message to Hitler appealing for him to give permission for the Afrika-Korps to withdraw, or face total destruction. The Führer immediately replied and told Rommel in no uncertain words that his forces were not to withdraw and must 'stand fast'.

In spite of the terrible situation, the Afrika-Korps fought on, and in some areas even to the death. But nothing could prevent the high losses and the gradual deterioration of the German forces. The British had fought brilliantly against the Afrika-Korps. Montgomery had wanted to fight a battle of attrition against his enemy, similar to those tactics used during the Great War. He had correctly predicted the outcome of the battle, leaving his great adversary to watch as entire units were smashed to pieces. 'If I stay here,' Rommel said, 'the army will not last more than a few days…If I do obey the Führer's order, then there will be a real danger that my own men will not obey me… My men come first.' With these words Rommel took the fate of the Afrika-Korps in his hands and ordered a massive retreat against Hitler's orders. The retreat would take his forces all the way into the

Tunisian highlands. But despite the withdrawal of the Afrika-Korps, Rommel was still seen as outwardly confident, even by the beginning of 1943, when defeat in the desert seemed a certainty.

A line of defences near Mersa El Brega in early 1942. It was along this line that German troops dug in and waited for word from Rommel to resume their ambitious drive across the desert.

Defensive positions near Mersa El Brega. During January 1942 Rommel decided he was going to launch a new attack from Mersa El Brega, capture Tobruk and carry the war towards Egypt. The 'Desert Fox' believed that he could smash the enemy quickly and decisively on the western border of Cyrenaica.

Troops dig in, in early 1942. Having chosen a suitable location, either for attack or defence against tanks or assault by a mobile column, soldiers would normally dig in and lay sandbags and cover their position with camouflage netting.

During a resting period one soldier shows his comrades a desert lizard he has found and places it on his left arm. Whilst spending short periods out of action the men generated their own forms of amusement.

A soldier poses for the camera next to his tent wearing just a pith helmet with goggles, a pair of shorts and ankle boots. Behind him the barren terrain can be seen stretching far away in the distance. When not on duty soldiers would often hide away in their tents as the scorching heat bore down on the dry, sandy terrain.

Two soldiers examine a downed British aircraft. By early 1942 the Germans were confronted by the marked superiority of the Royal Air Force. The RAF operated extensively in the ground fighting with strong forces almost without break. During 1942 they began to inflict massive losses on the Afrika Korps.

A Photograph showing General Cruwell, commander of the Afrika Korps, in March 1942.

Two officers confer with each other about the next move in the desert during the opening phase of Rommel's surprise attack in January 1942. The attack was launched on 21 January and almost immediately the Afrika Korps had outwitted and outgunned its enemy. Within five days the British were in full retreat, and the town of Benghazi had once more changed hands.

Two officers take the salute during a military ceremony. The troops in the background are all wearing the tropical sun helmet, or pith helmets. Although this headgear was discarded later in the campaign, they were still seen during parades and other formal occasions.

A soldier drives along a road outside the newly re-captured town of Benghazi. After the fall of Benghazi, Rommel reshuffled his Panzer army in order to prepare them for an attack on the British Gazala line.

A commanding officer makes alterations to his map, which is attached to a leather clipboard. He is seen wearing the tropical greatcoat and Afrika Korps field cap.

A variety of Panzers, consisting mainly of Pz.Kpfw.IIs and Pz.Kpfw.IIIs, are seen racing across the desert. German armoured units used various methods of advance, but the most common one used in the desert was the 'V' formation. This tactical formation was used in short rushes, taking full advantage of the terrain. Frequently, whole regiments moved in mass formation, with lines of tanks at regular intervals of about 60 – 70 feet, all advancing in waves.

An Sd.Kfz.251 halftrack has halted in the desert with three crew on board. The Sd.Kfz.251 halftrack was used extensively in North Africa. In the thick of battle they moved forward alongside the armour and providing it with valuable support. This halftrack is armed with an MG34 machine gun for local support.

Three vehicles have halted in the middle of the desert. On the right of the photograph is a Volkswagen Type 82 166 Kfz.1 cross-country light personnel carrier. In front of the Volkswagen is a Sd.Kfz.223. Behind both these vehicles is an early production Sd.Kfz.263 radio armoured car.

An Sd.Kfz.251 halftrack belonging to the 8th Panzer Regiment is transporting British prisoners to the rear. The halftrack proved a very useful supplement to the various vehicles that were utilised in North Africa and were used for many different tasks. Whilst in combat they could transport infantry to the forward edge of the battlefield, where they could disembark. Because the halftrack was relatively lightly armoured they could maintain speed with a good cross-country performance.

An Sd.Kfz.251 halftrack and a Pz.Kpfw.III have halted beside each other in the desert. Note on the tanks rear stowage bin, the Afrika Korps palm tree symbol, which was often painted in yellow with a swastika.

An officer and his driver from the 15th Panzer Division stop for a well-earned rest at the side of the road. The vehicle is filled with various items of equipment including the officer's suitcase. It is more than likely that this officer may have been re-posted to another unit, as it appears he has the majority of his belongings stowed in the boot.

Abandoned British positions. Rocks have helped construct a defensive position in the middle of the desert. Strewn around the defensive position are intact ammunition boxes, including an assortment of rifles and other pieces of equipment.

Whilst off duty, troops relax beneath a makeshift tent, trying their best to hide away from the scorching heat that bore down for hours every day on the dry sandy terrain.

A German commander poses with Italian officers. By February 1942 Rommel's Army was now designated Panzer Army Afrika. It included the 90th Light, 15th and 21st Panzer Divisions and seven Italian divisions, which were composed of the Pavia, Trento, Bologna, Brescia, Ariete and Sabratha.

An Sd.Kfz.251/1 Ausf.B passes a captured fortification in Cyrenaica. A German national flag can be seen attached over the front of the vehicle for aerial recognition. The halftrack has received a full application of yellow-brown, which was the official camouflage colour scheme of the Afrika Korps.

Four members of Rommel's staff can be seen conferring light-heartedly. In total Rommel's military staff consisted of some twenty-one officers.

Near the newly-captured town of Benghazi, off duty soldiers have taken a swim in the Mediterranean Sea and are getting dressed next to their Horch Cross Country vehicle.

A car has been utilised to carry provisions and other supplies for the Afrika Korps and has halted next to a well-erected tent. Sand bags, earth and rocks provide additional protection against the harsh desert environment. Attached to the entrance of the shelter is a waterproof Zeltbahn.

After being hit by an anti-tank round, the British Mk VI Crusader has burst into flames and black oily smoke billows from vehicle's inside compartment. The Mk VI Crusader was one of the least successful tanks in North Africa and was no match against the Pz.Kpfw.IV.

Posed photograph showing what appears to be an Arab or North African volunteer. During 1942 and 1943 the Vichy Government began recruiting Arabs, North Africans and even French citizens to support the Afrika Korps. By January 1943 there were almost 400 men enlisted.

A truck and motorcycle combination wind down a hillside. The motorcycle was used for both combat and reconnaissance roles and the Afrika Korps distributed literally hundreds of them among the Panzer and rifle regiments, flak detachments, artillery regiments, and reconnaissance units.

Hundreds of British troops are sprawled along the beach near Benghazi, waiting to be shipped to the rear as PoWs.

Afrika Korps troops on an airstrip are waiting to transport their sick and injured comrades on a Junker Ju52 transporter. The troops were normally flown back to Italy, but the injured far outweighed the replacements. However, after the capture of Benghazi, Derna and Martuba, the Luftwaffe was able to occupy landing strips, which increased air supplies and large quantities of reinforcements.

An old bus has been utilised as a temporary command post for these officers. Shelter was often at a premium in the desert and for this reason a multitude of vehicles were pressed into service by both the Afrika Korps and their Italian Allies.

Rommel salutes an officer as he passes to watch a formal ceremony, in which soldiers are receiving decoration for their bravery or marksmanship on the battlefield.

In the presence of Rommel a small formal parade of soldiers stand to attention with their Mauser rifles, to the salute of their commanding officer.

Rommel surveys the battlefield accompanied by some of his staff and Italian officers. The German officer to the right of Rommel is wearing the tropical greatcoat and has sewn on his right lower sleeve the 'AFRIKAKORPS' cuffband. The official cuff title was machine woven on a tan cloth band with a dark green central strip and aluminium weave bordering. The Afrika Korps lettering was always in block capitals and embroidered in aluminium metallic weave.

Three officers scrutinize a map during operations in 1942. The officer in the middle can be seen displaying the official Afrika Korps cuff title on the right lower sleeve of his tunic. Although the cuffbands were extensively used during the campaign, it was not always worn by troops, as many could not be bothered to stitch it to their tunics.

Four photographs showing familiar shots of Rommel leading his men from his staff car and consulting with staff about the general situation. From the front Rommel believed he had the best chance of infusing determination and courage into his forces. He was an active and energetic commander who kept his officers and troops on their toes. In front of his men he showed endless enthusiasm, drive and constant optimism. Any officer that did not share these beliefs was quickly removed and sent back to Germany. Out in his staff car travelling around the desert, Rommel had a stupendous drive to win at all costs.

It was on the battlefield leading his men that Rommel was able to use his own methods and ideas. He placed great emphasis on the use of mobile operations where speed, mobility, and long range were an essential ingredient to success. Sir Basil Liddell Hart wrote that Rommel was, by the standards of any war, an exceptionally talented and inspired leader of men – a great commander.

Two photographs taken in sequence minutes apart, showing a group of officers at a temporary command post in June 1942. During June the Afrika Korps continued combining artillery, infantry, tanks and close aerial support, with successful results. At Mersa Matruh they captured around 7,000 British troops of the 8th Army, and it seemed Alexandria was within their grasp with only 125 miles to go. However, the bulk of the 8th Army had fallen back to prepare much stronger defences further east. This was a bitter disappointment to Rommel who believed the bulk of the British forces had been trapped during the battle for Mersa Matruh.

A Pz.Kpfw.III advances through the desert. By the end of June the 90th Light Division reported it had reached Sidi Abd al-Rahman, only 20 miles west of El Alamein. The fall of Cairo was expected any day. The British, now demoralized, began preparing for the arrival of the Afrika Korps in Egypt. Defeat seemed imminent.

A photograph taken the moment a Pak gun opens fire against British positions during the summer of 1942. In spite of their impressive advance towards the Egyptian frontier, the Afrika Korps had only 55 tanks and was desperately in need of more troops. The Italians, however, were even worse off with only 5,500 infantry, 30 tanks and 200 guns. But despite his weakness, Rommel was determined to smash the British forces and use the 90th Light Division to cut the coast road before going in for the kill at El Alamein.

Dust and smoke is still visibly evident after the gun crew of a 15cm howitzer fires one of its shells against British positions during the battle of El Alamein. For a number of days the Germans pounded enemy positions as mobile units tried to take up primary positions. After days of intensive fighting Rommel lost many irreplaceable tanks and as a consequence the attack began to falter.

The desert is littered with wreckage during the battle of El Alamein. By early July British air activity had increased so much in the area that even Rommel himself was compelled to shelter in the ground for most of the day, like the majority of his troops.

Here Afrika Korps troops have captured a British Morris C8 4 x 4 'Quad' field artillery tractor, which can be seen towing a 25-pounder field gun.

The photograph captures the moment when the projectile leaves the artillery gun. The artillery commander has raised his arm signalling the gun crew to fire. Note the elevation of the gun barrel as it's used directly against advancing enemy ground forces.

A 15cm howitzer opens fire during intensive night-time attacks. During the first half of July the Afrika Korps more or less fought a bloody battle of attrition. For days German artillery pounded British positions, but still the British held on like grim death, in spite of their forces being thinly spread.

The first battle of El Alamein had been a British success. By the end of July Rommel's advance had been abruptly halted. During the fighting, though, both sides had incurred high casualties. In this photograph British prisoners pay their respects to their fallen comrades whilst a German soldier respectfully watches the brief ceremony.

A photograph of an Afrika Korps cemetery. In total Rommel's forces suffered 13,000 casualties during the first battle of El Alamein. These were losses that the Afrika Korps could not afford. By early August their stocks of troops, ammunition, tanks and supplies were critically low.

During a lull in the fighting 10.5cm howitzers can be seen prepared for action out in the desert, accompanied by a range of support vehicles. Though the 10.5cm howitzer was a highly regarded artillery piece, its maximum range was still limited, especially against the British 25-pounder.

A column of vehicles consisting of a Horch field staff car, which is leading an Sd.Kfz.263, followed by two Sd.Kfz.221 or 223 light armoured cars. The vehicle clearly displays the Afrika Korps palm tree symbol on the left fender. On the other fender it displays the white tactical sign for a reconnaissance unit.

A Pz.Kpfw.III has halted in the desert with one of its crew members resting on the front of the turret. The success of the Panzer in the desert depended entirely on its deployment en masse and the concentration of large numbers of tanks for a deep drive into enemy weak areas. However, by the second half of 1942, with the dwindling numbers of tanks, this tried and tested technique was unable to be used with full effect.

Soldiers stand next to a field kitchen. A field kitchen was a very important component to an infantry or Panzer division that had to endure the vast barren wasteland of the North African desert.

Here in this photograph one of the independent maintenance companies is undertaking some extensive work on a Pz.Kpfw.III, whilst the crew wait patiently in the shade, sitting on the tank's wheels. Much of the success of the Afrika Korps was owed to to their well-equipped maintenance companies, which kept the vehicles in fighting condition.

Chapter Five

Defeat in the Desert

During the third week of November 1942 the Afrika-Korps was in full retreat and had withdrawn through Benghazi. A month later it was embroiled in vicious fighting in Wadi Zem Zem, where German troops made a stand for almost three weeks before reaching Tripoli on 23 January 1943. By this stage of the campaign the Afrika-Korps was unlike the army that had first disembarked from the transport ships two years earlier. The Afrika-Korps was a shadow of its former self. To make matters worse the Anglo-America army had landed in Casablanca, Morocco, and Algiers. Montgomery's 8th Army now dominated the eastern coastline of Libya, whilst Eisenhower's 1st Army in Algeria and Morocco now occupied most of the coastline in the west. Already Hitler had dispatched the Hermann Göring Panzer Parachute and 334th Divisions, together constituting the 5th Panzer Army, which was moved westward to defend positions east of the Atlas Mountains against American forces. In January 1943 the 5th Panzer Army, commanded by General Jurgen von Arnim, had been given specific instructions to hold off a determined drive by the British 1st Army on Tunis and Bizerta. Already the 5th Panzer Army had undertaken a number of successful engagements, using its armoured strength to keep the enemy forces off balance. It had fought a series of battles against inexperienced American forces and weak French colonial troops at Fondouk, Bou Arada and Faid.

Whilst the 5th Panzer Army held its positions, Rommel had meanwhile been continuing the Afrika-Korps withdrawal across Libya into Tunisia and approached the Mareth Line via Tripoli. The Mareth Line stretched 22 miles inland from the sea to the Marmata hills, crossing the coastal road. It was a heavily defended area of fortifications that had been constructed initially by the French near the coastal town of Medenine in southern Tunisia prior to the war. It was primarily built to defend against attacks from the Italians in Libya, but was now in German hands. From an attacking position the Mareth Line was strategically unique. Rommel knew from these fortifications he could strike out at either or even both of the 1st and 8th Armies.

By late January 1943 Rommel prepared his forces, along with Arnim's 5th Panzer Army, to threaten the Allied position in Tunisia by unleashing a counterstroke. Although the Germans were strong enough to undertake such a bold attack, the mountainous terrain was less favourable for them. Almost as soon as the attack was unleashed, Panzer crews found that the valleys were often too narrow for their vehicles to force a passage through. However, between 14 and 17 February the 5th Panzer Army and Afrika-Korps launched a heavy armoured assault against the American II Corps. Around Sidi Bou Zid and Sbeitla, German and American forces clashed and scored a sizable success. In four days of heavy fighting the Americans had lost over 2,500 men, 280 vehicles, 103 tanks, 18 field guns, 3 anti-tank guns, and one anti-aircraft battery.

In order to avoid further slaughter the American II Corps hastily withdrew, but, between the 19 and 20 February, German massed armour once again struck out against the American II Corps, pushing the American forces back through the mountains at the Kasserine Pass into the valley beyond. As panic and confusion swept the American lines, the Germans took full advantage by smashing through abandoned enemy positions. Although further successes were beckoning for the Afrika-Korps, concerns about Montgomery's 8th Army approaching from Rommel's rear in Libya prompted him to halt the German drive west. Rommel ordered that his forces must return to Mareth to meet Montgomery's offensive, which he knew was being prepared against him.

On 26 February Arnim's 5th Panzer Army launched an attack against British forces in a drastic attempt to push its front west in order to enable German forces to hold a larger area around Tunis. Almost simultaneously, to the south, the Afrika-Korps were ordered to strike the British 8th Army at Medenine, but Panzers were soon brought to a flaming halt by massed artillery and anti-tank fire, supported by heavy aerial attacks. The Germans sustained massive losses. Two weeks later in mid-March the Anglo American forces went back over to the offensive. The British 8th Army then launched a breaching assault on the Mareth Line and by the 20 March managed to break through and drive back the old Panzer Army Afrika towards the Eastern Dorsal.

Over the next few weeks British forces managed to push back the Germans more than 150 miles and within 45 miles of Tunis. Despite the successful British drive, both German and Italian troops still boasted a considerable force in Tunisia. In total they fielded over eleven divisions with reinforcements, including remnants of the old Panzer Army Afrika. However, their supply situation was now worse than ever and as a consequence fuel was at a premium. Even the formidable Tiger tanks that had been rushed to Tunisia to counter the ever-increasing enemy armour suffered as the result of low fuel stocks. Those vehicles that could be used without the prospect of running out of fuel either became lost in swampy ground or were knocked out by Allied anti-tank guns. By the end of April the 5th Panzer Army was in a critical state. Only twenty-six tanks were reported to be still operational. In desperation some crews actually tried to distil fuel for their engines from fruit trees or from locally produced wines and spirits. If this was not enough, further supply problems manifested themselves as the Luftwaffe, confronted by an ever-increasing amount of enemy aircraft, abandoned Tunisia and flew to Italy. Slowly and systematically the 5th Panzer Army and the Afrika-Korps were ground down and soon confined to a small pocket covering Tunis and Bizerta. American forces, consisting of the 1st Armoured and 9th Infantry Divisions, co-ordinated an envelopment of Bizerta, and the following day, after intensive fighting, slowly pushed retreating German units through the town. Near Tunis, British forces subjected the German and Italians to merciless fighting as they prepared to smash their way through into the town. Both Tunis and Bizerta fell on 7 May. The 6th Armoured Division had the honour of capturing Tunis.

With the fall of Tunis, British rearguards maintained the pressure over the following week as remnants of Army Group Afrika, short of fuel and ammunition, frantically attempted to withdraw to safety to the coastal port town of Cape Bon. Its troops, now in a pitiful state, withdrew under the constant hammer blows of enemy artillery and continuous aerial attacks. The road to Cape Bon was remembered by many of the German survivors as the 'road of death'. Carnage and confusion filled the road, as troops scrambled in disorder to escape annihilation and reach what they thought would be sanctuary. But by 13 May with no more territory in which to defend, the last remnants of the Axis forces, consisting of some 275,000 soldiers including the German and Italian commanders, Arnim and General Messe, surrendered to the Allies.

The fall of North Africa was a complete disaster for the Germans and was the largest capitulation yet imposed by the Allies to date. As for Rommel, the great commander of the Afrika-Korps, he had taken sick leave and handed over his command on 9 March 1943 to Arnim. Presumably he was supposed to return after he had recovered, but knew he would never see Africa again. Rommel found his departure from the North African desert emotional as he said goodbye to his trusted staff. Sitting in his command vehicle, so often seen leading the Afrika-Korps into battle, he looked ill and exhausted. General Luck noticed tears in the 'Desert Fox's eyes as he handed him a memento photograph. For Rommel, he was leaving behind his beloved Afrika-Korps forever. He would have preferred that the Axis forces be evacuated with him than continuing to fight to the grim death and prolonging the inevitable wholesale destruction of his forces.

Nebeltruppen preparing their 15cm Nebelwerfer 41 for action in early 1943. This lethal weapon fired six 34kg Wurfgrenate 41 rockets. It took only ten seconds to fire a full salvo, but since the crew loaded it manually it could only fire three salvoes every five minutes. The Nebelwerfer was used against both the British and then American forces in North Africa with deadly effect.

A command post has been erected on the side of a rocky hillside. Note the amount of sand bags that have been used to protect the command centre against enemy attack.

The crew of an Sd.Kfz.251 and Pz.Kpfw.III keep a watchful eye before resuming their drive through the desert. For additional armoured protection the halftrack has a spare wheel bolted to the front, whilst the Panzer has spare track links festooned to the front.

A soldier has come across a dead Gazelle, which he has just hunted and killed. Rations in the Afrika Korps were often mundane and not very appetising. Apart from captured British bully beef, solders regularly welcomed freshly cooked succulent meat instead of tins of rations.

A soldier wearing a pith helmet can be seen collecting water from a hole. The water being collected is more than likely to be used for the radiator of the British captured Morris C8 4 x 4 quad field artillery tractor, which can seen in the background.

Out in the desert is a halted Volkswagen Type.82. Kfz.1. Its air-cooled engine enabled the car to operate very effectively in the heat of North Africa. The car was quick and well-built, and able to deal with all forms of terrain. It was used extensively, not only by the infantry for various supporting roles and reconnaissance, but also by officers.

Two photographs taken in sequence showing engineers extracting water from a water hole. The water was normally brought to the surface by pumps and other equipment. In this particular photograph the engineers are using a winch. Troops were very careful taking water from water wells that they came across, as they were fully aware that the British were very clever at polluting waterholes, wells or distillation plants with deadly chemicals.

A blurred photo showing troops of the Afrika Korps retreating through the desert in mid-January 1943. During this period the British 7th Armoured Division had broken through the German lines at Sirte and made a furious drive south towards Tarhuna. The Afrika Korps were now compelled to fall back. The road to Tripoli was wide open, and in spite of Hitler's frantic orders to hold the Libyan capital, Rommel reluctantly ordered the retreat to continue. The British finally marched into Tripoli on 23 January 1943.

Afrika Korps troops preparing their 15cm artillery gun for action against advancing British forces. In late January Rommel fell back on Tunisia, in the hope that his badly depleted forces could recover and build new lines of defence.

An artillery crew prepare their weapon for action. By late January 1943 the Afrika Korps had managed to co-ordinate their defences and counter-attacks against an enemy whose supply lines were now over-extended.

Here Afrika Korps troops examine the destroyed wreckage of a shot-down American P-38 Lightening in Tunisia. By early February 1943, American aerial attacks on German positions had escalated, causing considerable losses.

A Tiger tank has halted in the desert. There were three main Tiger battalions that were sent to North Africa and these consisted of the 501st, 503rd, and 504th Heavy Panzer Tiger Battalions. All three Tiger tank battalions saw extensive action in North Africa and played a number of prominent roles in various battles, demonstrating their awesome killing power.

An Sd.Kfz.251 command vehicle passes resting troops. In the distance black smoke indicates extensive fighting in the area. By the beginning of February there were no more than 126,000 German and Italian troops fighting in Tunisia. As for the American forces, they were lavishly supplied but were deficient in combat experience, which in turn helped the Afrika Korps win a number of decisive battles.

Three soldiers stand in front of a doorway of a building that has evidently seen some fighting. All the men wear the standard tropical greatcoat. The soldier on the right has been wounded in action as his head has been bandaged.

Tigers move along a road during operations in January or February 1943. These vehicles belong to the 501st Heavy Tiger Tank Battalion. The 501st was prepared for tropical deployment in late 1942 and initially fitted out with 20 Tigers. However, in spite a number of successful engagements, the 501st surrendered in Tunisia on 12 May. Its remnants were sent to the Eastern Front.

An 8.8cm flak gun mounted on its limber can be seen with its crew. When being used against ground targets, the 8.8cm flak gun was best suited to the North African terrain where it was often flat and open.

A gun layer peers through the gun sight, preparing his weapon to be fired against Amer positions in Tunisia. Between 14 and 17 February the 5th Panzer Army and Afrika Korps launche heavy armoured attack against the American II Corps, with German troops scoring a sizable succ

Three German officers pose for the camera in North Africa. Two of the officers wear the tropical cap with inverted 'V' Waffenfarbe, whilst the one in the centre has an M1938 grey-green field cap.

A light Horch cross-country vehicle moves quickly across the desert. The vehicle's canopy can clearly be seen raised to reduce the sun's rays penetrating down on the driver and passengers, and to prevent dust from entering the vehicle.

A German paratrooper or Fallschirmjäger soldier, camouflaged in a field of figs, peers through a pair of binoculars trying to deduce the location of the enemy. Although the Fallschirmjäger contribution to the North African campaign was not extensive, during the later part of the campaign in Tunisia units fought against overwhelming odds with great courage and determination. When the Axis war effort finally collapsed in May 1943, the bulk of the paratroopers were left behind and consequently found themselves as PoWs.

Local children run through the streets of Tunis, as Fallschirmjäger troops march through the town during their futile attempts to bolster the German force and keep the Allies out of French North Africa.

A temporary German defensive position out in Tunisia in April 1943. Scattered along the defensive line are a number of vehicles including a parked Pz.Kpfw.III. Over the coming weeks British forces managed to push back the Germans more than 150 miles and within 45 miles of Tunis.

A Luftwaffe field store out in the desert. By 1943 supplies were running drastically low for the German and Italian forces. Captured British and American stocks generally helped supplement the troops' meagre rations.

Here commanders of Army Group Afrika discuss the desperate situation in early 1943. The officers wear an assortment of clothing including the grey-green M1940 motorcyclists' greatcoat, M1940 continental greatcoat and British captured gear.

An officer instils courage and determination into his men during operations in Tunisia. The vehicle parked in the background is a 'Puma' Sd.Kfz.234/3 variant, mounting the 7.5cm KwK L/24 gun. This eight-wheeled vehicle was used mainly for reconnaissance duties.

A Volkswagen Kubelwagen is having trouble moving across the sand following a heavy downpour and is being given a helping hand by local natives during operations in Tunisia.

Commanders out in the desert discuss the general condition on the battlefield. By the end of February Rommel had only weak Italian divisions left holding their positions. Behind them, with some 10,000 German infantry, 150 tanks, and 190 guns, was the combined strength of the 10th, 15th and 21st Panzer Divisions. By this period the situation was less favourable than ever before.

A signals battalion during a brief respite. The soldiers are wearing the familiar tropical field cap, which is so bleached as to appear white against the contrasting colour of their dark-olive tunic.

Before resuming his drive, the commander of a Tiger tank belonging to the 501st Heavy Tiger tank Battalion surveys the battlefield using a pair of binoculars. The 501st was embroiled in thick fighting in North Africa and saw the last weeks bitterly contesting British armoured units in Tunisia until May 1943.

The local inhabitants of a town greet the arrival of a Marder.III belonging to the 15th Panzer Division. At the end of February 1943 this Marder was just one of a few remaining armoured vehicles that were used to hold the Mareth Line, with what was left of the once vaunted Afrika Korps and Axis forces.

Two photographs show war graves of German soldiers killed whilst fighting in North Africa. It is a visual reminder of the mass of life lost during the campaign. These war graves undoubtedly mark the last resting place of those who paid the supreme sacrifice for their country between February 1941 and May 1943.

Chapter Six

Afrika-Korps Uniforms

When it appeared that German forces would be used in North Africa in early 1941, manufacturers quickly began designing an army tropical field service uniform. The uniform was made of lightweight canvas drill, dyed either in a sand tan or light green colour. After weeks of use in the desert the combination of high temperatures and the penetrating sunrays altered the colour of the uniform to a much lighter appearance. The style of the tropical field tunic was almost identical to the design of the M1936 Army service uniform, but it was made from lightweight cotton drill. It had four box-pleated pockets, but the German national emblem positioned above the right breast pocket was woven in golden-yellow artificial silk on a tan cloth backing. As for the collar patch, this was a special tropical version intended to be worn by all ranks and was woven in a pale blue-grey artificial silk on a copper brown backing. Another variation of the tropical tunic was the variety of uniform insignia worn. The first unofficial type was known as the 'Afrikakorps' cuffband, which was machine embroidered in sliver-grey block letters on black cloth and sewn onto the bottom of the right arm. The official 'Afrikakorps' cuffband was woven in aluminium thread on a dark green/tan background. Another Afrikakorps cuffband was the 'Afrika' campaign cuff title. This was machine embroidered in silver-grey thread on a medium brown camel-hair material. The braid edging was also sliver grey.

When the soldiers were not wearing the tropical tunic they were seen in the German Army tropical shirt, which was generally a replacement for the tropical Army tunic during operations in the desert. The shirt was very similar in design to that of the field-grey shirt worn by the Army in Europe and Russia. It had two breast pockets, both with button-down flaps. The shirt was long-sleeved and was not buttoned completely down, which forced the wearer to remove the garment by pulling it over his head. The shirt was made of hard-wearing cotton drill, dyed to a dark sand colour, but again was bleached to a much lighter colour by the harsh climate of the North African sun.

The lightweight trousers worn with either the tropical shirt or tunic were again very similar to the design of the M1936 Army service uniform, although there were a number of variations. One variation included the soldier wearing shorts. This not only allowed the wearer to move more freely across sandy terrain, but also kept him considerably cooler during the high daytime temperatures. Both trousers and shorts were worn with leather high-lace-up tropical boots. The long tropical trousers were usually worn gathered in around the ankles of the boots.

The tropical field service uniform was generally worn by all ranks. Army Generals wore the tropical jacket version and the features of the design were almost identical to all those found on officers wearing the M1936 Army field service uniform in Europe and Russian theatres of war. However, there was a slight variation with the tropical jacket, with it having plain sleeve ends without the normal deep turn-back cuffs.

Often worn over the Afrika-Korps uniform, especially during adverse weather conditions, was the army greatcoat. This garment was especially designed for wear out in North Africa and was known as the Afrika-Korps khaki greatcoat. This was very similar in design to the standard army pattern greatcoat, but was produced as a tropical greatcoat of heavy brown wool, to prevent the wearer from the cold of the desert night.

Headgear

In the vast sprawling desert of North Africa, German troops were fighting a completely different type of warfare. Not only was the terrain and climate dissimilar but also the forms of headdress were adapted differently to cope with climate and blend in with the local terrain. The main form of headdress worn in North Africa was the tropical headdress. In February 1941, when the first German soldiers were sent to North Africa, all ranks wore the army sun helmet. The sun helmet or pith helmet was cork covered with olive canvas. It had a leather strap and binding. On the right side it had an embossed plate or shield displaying the national tricolour of black, white and red. The shield on the left side bore a dull silver metal Wehrmacht adler raised from a black painted shield.

Although mass produced and issued to the troops in North Africa, the pith helmet was not a very popular piece of headdress among the men. It was regarded not only as an awkward piece of headgear, but its actual value in terms of a protective headdress was doubtful. In view of its unpopularity, by late 1941 the pith helmet was phased out. In its place German soldiers took to wearing the Afrika-Korps field cap. This cap was designed prior to the general service headdress worn by the German Army and became the best-known item of tropical field dress. It was made in lightweight cotton drill and its material was dark olive in colour, which could vary towards either brown, or green with fading. The cap had a machine-woven national emblem, which was positioned on the front in pale blue-grey, and the flat machine-woven national cockade sewn on a diamond of tan backing.

Another popular item of headdress worn by the Afrika-Korps was the M1935 steel helmet. This headgear had been designed primarily to protect the head and neck whilst under combat conditions. Generally the steel helmets issued to all German soldiers were usually field-grey in colour and were manufactured either in matt or semi-matt finishes. However, in hotter climates like North Africa, Italy and even during the summer months in southern Russia, soldiers over-painted their steel helmets in a sand base colour.

For the remainder of the war until the spring of 1943, the Afrika-Korps field cap and the M1935 steel helmet, together with the M1938 field cap, became the main items of headdress worn by the Afrika-Korps.

Chapter Seven

Order of Battle

Panzer Gruppen Afrika

September 1941

German Afrika Korps
German 15th Panzer Division
Italian XXI Corps

Panzer Armee Afrika

January 1942

German Afrika Korps
German 90th Light Africa Division
Italian X Corps
Italian XXI Corps
Italian Corpo d'Armata di Manovra
Italian 55th Division Savona

April 1942

German Afrika Korps
German 90th Light Africa Division
Italian X Corps
Italian XX Motorized Corps
Italian XXI Corps

August 1942

German Afrika Korps
Italian X Corps
Italian XX Motorized Corps
Italian XXI Corps
Italian 133rd Armored Division Littorio

German-Italian Panzer Armee

November 1942

German Afrika Korps
German 90th Light Afrika Division
Italian X Corps
Italian XX Motorized Corps
Italian XXI Corps
Italian 136th Motorized Infantry Division
Italian 17th Infantry Division Pavia

February 1943

German Afrika Korps
German 164th Light Afrika Division
German Ramcke Parachute Brigade
Italian XX Motorized Corps
Italian XXI Corps

February 1943

German Fifth Panzer Army [Operations in northern Tunisia)
Italian First Army [Operations in southern Tunisia]